All New!

CHURCH *suppers*

W9-AFZ-869

pil

Publications International, Ltd.

Copyright © 2011 Publications International, Ltd.
All rights reserved. This publication may not be reproduced or quoted in whole or in part by any means whatsoever without written permission from:

Louis Weber, CEO
Publications International, Ltd.
7373 North Cicero Avenue
Lincolnwood, IL 60712

Permission is never granted for commercial purposes.

Favorite Brand Name Recipes is a trademark of Publications International, Ltd.

All recipes and photographs that contain specific brand names are copyrighted by those companies and/or associations, unless otherwise specified. All photographs *except* those on pages 13, 15, 23, 43, 57 and 71 copyright © Publications International, Ltd.

Campbell's® and Swanson® registered trademarks of CSC Brands LP. All rights reserved.

LOUIS RICH® is a registered trademark of Oscar Mayer Foods Corporation.

Carnation, Nestlé and Toll House are registered trademarks of Nestlé.

Pepperidge Farm® registered trademark of Pepperidge Farm, Incorporated. All rights reserved.

Some of the products listed in this publication may be in limited distribution.

Scripture quotations marked (NIV) are from the Holy Bible, New International Version®, NIV®. Copyright © 1973, 1978, 1984 by Biblica, Inc.™ Used by permission of Zondervan. All rights reserved worldwide. www.zondervan.com.

Scripture quotations marked (NRSV) are from the New Revised Standard Version Bible, copyright © 1989 National Council of the Churches of Christ in the United States of America. Used by permission. All rights reserved.

Pictured on the front cover: Baked Gnocchi *(page 34)*.
Pictured on the back cover: *(clockwise from top left):* Carrot Raisin Salad *(page 88)*, Old-Fashioned Meat Loaf *(page 6)* and Sweet Potato Pecan Pie *(page 138)*.

ISBN-13: 978-1-4508-4232-7
ISBN-10: 1-4508-4232-1

Library of Congress Control Number: 2011922739

Manufactured in China.

8 7 6 5 4 3 2 1

Microwave Cooking: Microwave ovens vary in wattage. Use the cooking times as guidelines and check for doneness before adding more time.

Preparation/Cooking Times: Preparation times are based on the approximate amount of time required to assemble the recipe before cooking, baking, chilling or serving. These times include preparation steps such as measuring, chopping and mixing. The fact that some preparations and cooking can be done simultaneously is taken into account. Preparation of optional ingredients and serving suggestions is not included.

Publications International, Ltd.

contents

Crispy Ranch Chicken

1½ cups crushed cornflakes
  1 teaspoon dried rosemary
  ½ teaspoon salt
  ½ teaspoon black pepper
1½ cups ranch salad dressing
  3 pounds chicken pieces

1. Preheat oven to 375°F. Spray 13×9-inch baking dish with nonstick cooking spray. Combine crushed cornflakes, rosemary, salt and pepper in medium bowl.

2. Pour salad dressing in separate medium bowl. Dip chicken pieces in salad dressing, coating well. Dredge coated chicken in cornflake mixture. Place in prepared baking dish.

3. Bake 50 to 55 minutes or until cooked through (165°F).

Makes 6 servings

To add an Italian flair to this dish, try substituting
1¼ cups Italian-seasoned dry bread crumbs and
¼ cup grated Parmesan cheese for the crushed
cornflakes, rosemary, salt and pepper. Prepare
the recipe as directed.

Crispy Ranch Chicken

Old-Fashioned Meat Loaf

1 teaspoon olive oil
1 cup finely chopped onion
4 cloves garlic, minced
1½ pounds ground beef
1 cup chili sauce, divided
¾ cup old-fashioned oats
2 egg whites
½ teaspoon black pepper
¼ teaspoon salt
1 tablespoon Dijon mustard

1. Preheat oven to 375°F. Heat oil in large nonstick skillet over medium heat. Add onion; cook and stir 5 minutes. Add garlic; cook and stir 1 minute. Transfer to large bowl; cool 5 minutes.

2. Add beef, ½ cup chili sauce, oats, egg whites, pepper and salt to bowl; mix well. Pat into 9×5-inch loaf pan. Combine remaining ½ cup chili sauce and mustard in small bowl; spoon evenly over top of meat loaf.

3. Bake 45 to 50 minutes or until cooked through (160°F). Let stand 5 minutes. Pour off any juices from pan. Cut into slices.

Makes 6 servings

Chicken Mozzarella

4 skinless, boneless chicken breasts halves (about 1 pound)
1 can (10¾ ounces) CAMPBELL'S® Healthy Request® Condensed Tomato Soup
½ teaspoon dried Italian seasoning or dried oregano leaves
½ teaspoon garlic powder
¼ cup shredded mozzarella cheese
3 cups corkscrew-shaped pasta, cooked without salt and drained

1. Place the chicken into a 2-quart shallow baking dish. Stir the soup, Italian seasoning and garlic powder in a small bowl. Spoon the soup mixture over the chicken.

2. Bake at 400°F. for 20 minutes or until the chicken is cooked through. Sprinkle with the cheese. Let stand for 5 minutes. Serve the chicken and sauce with the pasta.

Makes 4 servings

Old-Fashioned Meat Loaf

Mustard, Garlic and Herb Roasted Turkey Breast

¼ cup chopped fresh parsley
¼ cup spicy brown mustard
2 tablespoons chopped fresh thyme *or* 2 teaspoons dried thyme
2 tablespoons chopped fresh sage *or* 2 teaspoons dried sage
2 cloves garlic, minced
½ teaspoon black pepper
¼ teaspoon salt
1 bone-in whole turkey breast (6 to 7 pounds)

1. Preheat oven to 450°F. Combine parsley, mustard, thyme, sage, garlic, pepper and salt in medium bowl; mix well.

2. Loosen skin from turkey breast by inserting fingers and gently pushing between skin and meat. Rub mustard mixture under loosened skin, distributing mixture evenly over breast. Place turkey on rack in shallow roasting pan.

3. Place turkey in oven and immediately reduce oven temperature to 325°F. Roast 2 to 2½ hours or until internal temperature reaches 165°F. Transfer turkey to cutting board. Tent with foil; let stand 10 minutes before slicing.

Makes 8 to 10 servings

Fresh herbs are very perishable, so purchase them in small amounts. For short-term storage, place the herb stems in water. Cover the leaves loosely with a plastic bag or plastic wrap and store in the refrigerator. They will last from two days (basil, chives, dill, mint, oregano) to five days (rosemary, sage, tarragon, thyme).

Mustard, Garlic and Herb Roasted
Turkey Breast

Speedy Salmon Patties

1 can (12 ounces) pink salmon, undrained
1 egg, lightly beaten
¼ cup minced green onions
1 tablespoon chopped fresh dill
1 clove garlic, minced
½ cup all-purpose flour
1½ teaspoons baking powder
1½ cups vegetable oil

1. Drain salmon, reserving 2 tablespoons liquid. Place salmon in medium bowl; break apart with fork. Add reserved liquid, egg, green onions, dill and garlic; mix well.

2. Combine flour and baking powder in small bowl; add to salmon mixture. Stir until well blended. Shape mixture into six patties.

3. Heat oil in large heavy skillet. Add salmon patties; cook until golden brown on both sides. Remove from oil; drain on paper towels. Serve warm.

Makes 6 patties

Tortilla Crunch Chicken Fingers

1 envelope LIPTON® RECIPE SECRETS® Savory Herb with Garlic Soup Mix
1 cup finely crushed plain tortilla chips or cornflakes (about 3 ounces)
1½ pounds boneless, skinless chicken breasts, cut into strips
1 egg
2 tablespoons water
2 tablespoons I CAN'T BELIEVE IT'S NOT BUTTER!® Spread, melted

1. Preheat oven to 400°F.

2. In medium bowl, combine soup mix and tortilla chips. In large plastic bag or bowl, combine chicken and egg beaten with water until evenly coated. Remove chicken and dip in tortilla mixture until evenly coated; discard bag. On 15½×10½×1-inch jelly-roll pan sprayed with nonstick cooking spray, arrange chicken; drizzle with I Can't Believe It's Not Butter!® Spread. Bake uncovered, 12 minutes or until chicken is thoroughly cooked. Serve, if desired, with chunky salsa.

Makes about 24 chicken fingers

Beef Tenderloin with Easy Cranberry Balsamic Sauce

    1 whole beef tenderloin roast (about 4 to 5 pounds)
    2 tablespoons chopped fresh thyme
    1 tablespoon black pepper
    ⅓ cup balsamic vinegar
    3 tablespoons finely chopped shallots
    1 can (16 ounces) whole berry cranberry sauce
    ¼ teaspoon salt

1. Heat oven to 425°F. Combine thyme and pepper; reserve 1 teaspoon seasoning mixture for sauce. Press remaining seasoning mixture evenly onto all surfaces of beef roast.

2. Place roast on rack in shallow roasting pan. Insert ovenproof meat thermometer so tip is centered in thickest part of beef. Do not add water or cover. Roast in 425°F oven 50 to 60 minutes for medium rare; 60 to 70 minutes for medium doneness.

3. Remove roast when meat thermometer registers 135°F for medium rare; 150°F for medium. Transfer roast to carving board; tent loosely with aluminum foil. Let stand 15 to 20 minutes. (Temperature will continue to rise about 10°F to reach 145°F for medium rare; 160°F for medium.)

4. Meanwhile, prepare sauce. Combine vinegar and shallots in small saucepan; bring to a boil. Reduce heat; simmer 3 minutes. Stir in cranberry sauce; bring to a boil. Reduce heat; simmer 6 minutes to blend flavors, stirring occasionally. Remove from heat; stir in reserved seasoning and salt.

5. Carve roast into slices; serve with sauce.   *Makes 8 to 10 servings*

Favorite recipe from **Courtesy The Beef Checkoff**

Beef Tenderloin with Easy Cranberry
Balsamic Sauce

Herbed Pork Roast & Creamy Mushroom Gravy

1 teaspoon each minced fresh rosemary leaves, parsley leaves and thyme leaves or ¼ teaspoon each dried rosemary leaves, parsley flakes and thyme leaves, crushed

1 clove garlic, minced

1 boneless pork loin roast (2½ to 3 pounds)

1 can (10¾ ounces) CAMPBELL'S® Condensed Cream of Mushroom Soup (Regular or 98% Fat Free)

½ cup water

1. Stir the rosemary, parsley, thyme and garlic in a small bowl. Cut small slits into the surface of the pork with a knife. Stuff the herb mixture into the slits. Place the pork into a roasting pan.

2. Bake at 325°F. for 1 hour 30 minutes or until the pork is cooked through. Remove the pork from the pan and let stand for 10 minutes.

3. Stir the soup and water in the roasting pan. Cook and stir over medium heat until the mixture is hot and bubbling, scraping up the browned bits from the bottom of the pan. Serve the pork with the gravy.

Makes 8 servings

Kitchen Tip: If you're using dried herbs in this recipe, make sure to crush them before using. It releases the oils and, therefore, the flavor.

Go, eat your food with gladness, and drink . . .
with a joyful heart.   Ecclesiastes 9:7 NIV

Herbed Pork Roast &
Creamy Mushroom Gravy

Game-Winning Drumsticks

15 chicken drumsticks (about 4 pounds)
1¾ cups SWANSON® Chicken Stock
½ cup Dijon-style mustard
⅓ cup Italian-seasoned dry bread crumbs

1. Place the chicken in a single layer into a 15×9-inch disposable foil pan.

2. Stir the stock and mustard in a small bowl. Pour the stock mixture over the chicken and turn to coat. Sprinkle the bread crumbs over the chicken. Cover the pan and refrigerate for 4 hours.

3. Bake at 375°F. for 1 hour or until the chicken is cooked through. Serve hot or at room temperature.   *Makes 6 servings*

Kitchen Tip: Keep disposable foil pans on hand for convenience to tote casseroles to friends' parties or covered-dish suppers. As a safety reminder, be sure to support the bottom of the filled pan when handling them in and out of the oven.

Cranberry-Glazed Ham

1 fully cooked spiral-sliced ham half (5 to 6 pounds)*
¾ cup cranberry sauce or cranberry chutney
¼ cup Dijon mustard
1 teaspoon ground cinnamon
¼ teaspoon ground allspice

*A whole ham is usually 10 to 12 pounds and serves 24. Double the glaze ingredients if using a whole ham.

1. Preheat oven to 300°F. Place ham in large roasting pan lined with heavy-duty foil. Combine cranberry sauce, mustard, cinnamon and allspice; stir until well blended. Spread half of mixture evenly over top of ham. (Glaze will melt and spread as it cooks.)

2. Bake 1 hour; spread remaining cranberry mixture over top of ham. Bake about 1 hour or until internal temperature of ham reaches 140°F. Transfer ham to cutting board; let stand 5 minutes before serving.
Makes 10 to 12 servings

Garlic-Herb Crusted Beef Roast

1 boneless beef round rump roast *or* **beef bottom round roast**
    (3 to 4 pounds)
   Salt and ground black pepper

Rub:
   2 teaspoons garlic-pepper seasoning
   2 teaspoons dried basil leaves
   2 teaspoons dried thyme leaves
   1 teaspoon dried parsley leaves

1. Heat oven to 325°F. Combine rub ingredients in small bowl; press evenly onto all surfaces of beef roast.

2. Place roast on rack in shallow roasting pan. Insert ovenproof meat thermometer so tip is centered in thickest part of beef, not resting in fat. Do not add water or cover. Roast in 325°F oven 1½ to 2 hours for medium rare doneness.

3. Remove roast when meat thermometer registers 135°F for medium rare. Transfer roast to carving board; tent loosely with aluminum foil. Let stand 15 to 20 minutes. (Temperature will continue to rise about 10°F to reach 145°F for medium rare.)

4. Carve roast into thin slices; season with salt and black pepper, as desired.

Makes 6 to 8 servings

Favorite recipe from **Courtesy The Beef Checkoff**

Always carve roasts and large pieces of meat across the grain to prevent stringiness and to ensure tenderness. To identify the grain, look for long thin parallel fibers along the meat and slice across them.

Crisp Lemony Baked Fish

1¼ cups crushed cornflakes
¼ cup shredded Parmesan cheese
2 tablespoons minced green onions (green parts only)
⅛ teaspoon black pepper
1 lemon
1 egg
4 small haddock fillets (about 3 ounces each)

1. Preheat oven to 400°F. Line baking sheet with parchment paper.

2. Combine crushed cornflakes, Parmesan cheese, green onions and pepper on large plate. Grate lemon peel; stir into cornflake mixture. Reserve lemon.

3. Beat egg in shallow bowl. Dip fish fillets into egg, then into cornflake mixture; coat well on both sides. Place coated fillets on prepared baking sheet.

4. Bake about 10 minutes or until fish begins to flake when tested with fork. Cut reserved lemon into wedges; serve with fish.

Makes 4 servings

*To keep your hands from becoming breaded too, use
one hand to dip the fish fillets into the egg and the
other hand to coat them with the cornflake mixture.*

Roasted Turkey Breast with Herbed au Jus

1 tablespoon all-purpose flour

1 plastic oven bag, turkey size

1 cup SWANSON® Chicken Stock

½ teaspoon each ground dried sage leaves, dried rosemary and thyme leaves, crushed

1 (6- to 8-pound) bone-in turkey breast

½ teaspoon paprika (optional)

1 can (10½ ounces) CAMPBELL'S® Turkey Gravy

1. Add the flour to the oven bag. Close and shake the bag to distribute the flour. Place the bag in a 13×9×2-inch baking pan. Add the stock, sage, rosemary and thyme to the bag. Squeeze the bag to blend in the flour.

2. Rinse the turkey with cold water and pat dry with a paper towel. Sprinkle the turkey evenly with the paprika. Add the turkey to the bag. Close the bag with the nylon tie. Cut 6 (½-inch) slits in the top of the bag. Insert a meat thermometer through a slit in the bag into the thickest part of the meat, making sure the thermometer is not touching the bone.

3. Roast the turkey at 350°F. for 1¾ to 2 hours.* Begin checking for doneness after 1½ hours of roasting time. Let the turkey stand for 10 minutes before slicing.

4. Remove the turkey from the bag. Pour the turkey liquid from bag into large cup. Skim off the fat.

5. Heat the turkey liquid and gravy in a 2-quart saucepan over medium heat until hot. Serve with the turkey.   *Makes 6 servings*

*The internal temperature of the turkey should reach 170°F.

Roasted Turkey Breast with Herbed au Jus

Pineapple Apricot Glazed Ham

1 can (20 ounces) DOLE® Pineapple Slices
1 (5½- to 7-pound) ham
   Whole cloves
1 cup apricot jam or pineapple-apricot jam, divided
2 tablespoons balsamic or red wine vinegar
2 tablespoons honey
1 teaspoon cornstarch
⅛ teaspoon ground cinnamon

• Drain pineapple; reserve ¾ cup juice. Chop 4 pineapple slices into small pieces; set aside.

• Score top of ham in diamond pattern, making ¼-inch-deep cuts. Insert cloves into each diamond. Place in shallow baking pan. Brush with ¼ cup jam; cover with foil.

• Bake ham according to package directions. Arrange 6 pineapple slices on top of ham during the last 30 minutes of baking. Brush pineapple and ham with another ¼ cup jam and continue baking.

• Combine reserved juice, vinegar, honey, cornstarch, cinnamon and remaining ½ cup jam in medium saucepan. Bring to boil. Reduce heat; cook and stir 2 minutes or until slightly thickened.

• Stir chopped pineapple into sauce; heat through. Serve warm over ham slices. *Makes 16 servings*

They broke bread in their homes and ate together
with glad and sincere hearts.   *Acts 2:46 NIV*

Oven Barbecue Chicken

1 cup barbecue sauce
¼ cup honey
2 tablespoons soy sauce
2 teaspoons grated fresh ginger
½ teaspoon dry mustard
1 chicken, cut up (about 3½ pounds)

1. Preheat oven to 350°F. Grease 13×9-inch baking dish. Combine barbecue sauce, honey, soy sauce, ginger and mustard in small bowl; mix well.

2. Place chicken in prepared baking dish. Brush evenly with sauce mixture.

3. Bake 45 minutes or until cooked through (165°F), brushing occasionally with sauce. *Makes 4 to 6 servings*

Spicy-Sweet Brisket

4 to 5 pounds boneless beef brisket, well trimmed
1 pound fresh mushrooms, cleaned but not sliced
3 carrots, cut into 2-inch pieces
3 onions, thinly sliced
1 rib celery, cut into 2-inch pieces
1 (26-ounce) jar NEWMAN'S OWN® Diavolo Sauce
½ cup water
½ cup packed brown sugar
1 tablespoon garlic powder
½ teaspoon black pepper

Preheat oven to 350°F. Brown meat in large ungreased skillet. Remove to large Dutch oven. Add vegetables to meat. In separate bowl, combine Diavolo Sauce, water and brown sugar; stir and pour over meat. Sprinkle with garlic powder and pepper.

Cover tightly and bake 3 hours. Remove cover and allow meat to slightly brown 30 minutes.

Brisket should be made a day ahead of time and refrigerated overnight to allow flavors to blend. Thinly slice brisket across the grain.

Makes 12 servings

Oven Barbecue Chicken

Turkey Pot Pie Casserole

2 pounds turkey breast, cut into 1-inch cubes
6 tablespoons butter
⅓ cup all-purpose flour
½ teaspoon ground sage
½ teaspoon ground thyme
1½ cups chicken broth
1 cup milk
1 package (16 ounces) frozen soup vegetables (carrots, potatoes, peas, celery, green beans, corn, onions and lima beans)
1 teaspoon salt
½ teaspoon black pepper
1 can (8 ounces) refrigerated crescent roll dough

1. Preheat oven to 375°F. Spray 13×9-inch baking dish with nonstick cooking spray.

2. Spray large nonstick skillet with nonstick cooking spray; heat over medium heat. Working in batches, brown turkey on all sides. Transfer to large bowl

3. Melt butter in same skillet. Whisk in flour, sage and thyme; cook and stir 5 minutes. Slowly whisk in broth and milk; cook, whisking constantly, about 5 minutes or until thickened.

4. Stir in turkey, vegetables, salt and pepper; cook 5 to 7 minutes or until thick and creamy, stirring frequently. Spoon mixture into prepared baking dish. Unroll crescent roll dough; place over turkey mixture. Bake 15 minutes or until golden brown. *Makes 6 servings*

Country Sausage Macaroni and Cheese

   1 pound BOB EVANS® Special Seasonings Roll Sausage
1½ cups milk
 12 ounces pasteurized processed Cheddar cheese, cut into cubes
 ½ cup Dijon mustard
  1 cup diced fresh or drained canned tomatoes
  1 cup sliced mushrooms
⅓ cup sliced green onions
⅛ teaspoon cayenne pepper
 12 ounces uncooked elbow macaroni
  2 tablespoons grated Parmesan cheese

Preheat oven to 350°F. Crumble and cook sausage in medium skillet until browned. Drain on paper towels. Combine milk, processed cheese and mustard in medium saucepan; cook and stir over low heat until cheese melts and mixture is smooth. Stir in sausage, tomatoes, mushrooms, green onions and cayenne pepper. Remove from heat.

Cook macaroni according to package directions; drain. Combine hot macaroni and cheese mixture in large bowl; toss until well coated. Spoon into greased shallow 2-quart casserole dish. Cover and bake 15 to 20 minutes. Stir; sprinkle with Parmesan cheese. Bake, uncovered, 5 minutes more. Let stand 10 minutes before serving. Refrigerate leftovers.

Makes 6 to 8 servings

Chili powders, ground red pepper (cayenne) and red pepper flakes are all made from dried chiles. Whether you're working with fresh, dried or ground chiles, it is important to know that the longer you cook them, the hotter the dish will be. That's why a long simmered stew with chiles may be quite hot, while a quick stir-fry with chiles has more flavor and less heat.

Tuna Noodle Casserole

2 cups uncooked elbow macaroni
2 tablespoons butter
¾ cup chopped onion (½ large onion)
½ cup thinly sliced celery (2 stalks)
½ cup finely chopped red bell pepper
2 tablespoons all-purpose flour
½ teaspoon salt
⅛ teaspoon white pepper
1½ cups milk
1 can (6 ounces) albacore tuna in water, drained
½ cup grated Parmesan cheese, divided

1. Preheat oven to 375°F. Spray 8-inch square baking dish with nonstick cooking spray.

2. Cook pasta according to package directions; drain and set aside.

3. Meanwhile, melt butter in large deep skillet over medium heat. Add onion; cook and stir 3 minutes. Add celery and bell pepper; cook and stir 3 minutes. Add flour, salt and white pepper to vegetables; cook and stir 1 minute. Gradually stir in milk; bring to a boil. Cook and stir 2 minutes or until thickened. Remove from heat.

4. Add pasta, tuna and ¼ cup Parmesan cheese to skillet; stir until pasta is well coated. Pour tuna mixture into prepared dish; sprinkle evenly with remaining ¼ cup Parmesan cheese.

5. Bake, uncovered, 20 to 25 minutes or until hot and bubbly.

Makes 4 servings

*It is God's gift that all should eat and drink and take
pleasure in all their toil.   Ecclesiastes 3:13 NRSV*

Ham and Swiss Quiche

1 cup (4 ounces) shredded Swiss cheese, divided
1 cup finely chopped cooked ham
2 green onions, sliced
1 *unbaked* 9-inch (4-cup volume) deep-dish pie shell
1 can (12 fluid ounces) NESTLÉ® CARNATION® Evaporated Milk
3 large eggs
¼ cup all-purpose flour
¼ teaspoon salt
⅛ teaspoon ground black pepper

PREHEAT oven to 350°F.

SPRINKLE ½ cup cheese, ham and green onions into pie shell. Whisk together evaporated milk, eggs, flour, salt and pepper in large bowl. Pour mixture into pie shell; sprinkle with remaining cheese.

BAKE for 45 to 50 minutes or until knife inserted near center comes out clean. Cool on wire rack for 10 minutes before serving.

Makes 8 servings

Lattice-Top Quiche: Use ready-made pie pastry for single crust pie. Cut pastry into ½-inch-wide strips. Lay pastry strips over filling in lattice fashion, turning pastry over outside edge of dish. Bake as directed above.

May this meal nourish our busy bodies as the anticipation of God's presence among us does our weary spirits.

Baked Gnocchi

1 package (about 17 ounces) gnocchi
⅓ cup olive oil
3 cloves garlic, minced
1 package (10 ounces) frozen spinach, thawed and squeezed dry
1 can (about 14 ounces) diced tomatoes
1 teaspoon Italian seasoning
   Salt and black pepper
½ cup grated Parmesan cheese
½ cup (2 ounces) shredded mozzarella cheese

1. Preheat oven to 350°F. Grease 2½-quart casserole or gratin dish.

2. Cook gnocchi according to package directions; drain and set aside.

3. Meanwhile, heat oil in large skillet or Dutch oven over medium heat. Add garlic; cook and stir 30 seconds. Stir in spinach; cook, covered, 2 minutes or until spinach wilts. Add tomatoes and Italian seasoning. Season with salt and pepper; cook and stir about 5 minutes. Add gnocchi; stir gently.

4. Transfer gnocchi mixture to prepared casserole. Sprinkle with cheeses. Bake 20 to 30 minutes or until casserole is bubbly and cheese is melted.

Makes 4 to 6 servings

Mom's Best Chicken Tetrazzini

8 ounces uncooked thin noodles or vermicelli
2 tablespoons butter
8 ounces fresh mushrooms, sliced
¼ cup chopped green onions
1 can (about 14 ounces) chicken broth
1 cup half-and-half, divided
2 tablespoons dry sherry
¼ cup all-purpose flour
½ teaspoon salt
¼ teaspoon ground nutmeg
⅛ teaspoon white pepper
1 jar (2 ounces) chopped pimiento, drained
½ cup grated Parmesan cheese, divided
½ cup sour cream
2 cups cubed cooked chicken

1. Preheat oven to 350°F. Spray 1½-quart casserole with nonstick cooking spray. Cook pasta according to package directions; drain and set aside.

2. Meanwhile, melt butter in large nonstick skillet over medium-high heat. Add mushrooms and green onions; cook and stir until green onions are tender. Add chicken broth, ½ cup half-and-half and sherry to onion mixture.

3. Pour remaining ½ cup half-and-half into small jar with tight-fitting lid; add flour, salt, nutmeg and pepper. Shake well.

4. Slowly stir flour mixture into skillet. Bring to a boil; cook 1 minute. Reduce heat; stir in pimiento and ¼ cup Parmesan cheese. Stir in sour cream; mix well. Add chicken and noodles; mix well.

5. Spread mixture evenly into prepared casserole. Sprinkle with remaining ¼ cup Parmesan cheese. Bake 30 to 35 minutes or until hot.

Makes 6 servings

Diner Special Meatloaf

  1 pound lean ground beef
½ cup KRAFT® Original Barbecue Sauce
½ cup dry bread crumbs
  1 egg, lightly beaten
1¼ cups water
¾ cup milk
  2 tablespoons butter or margarine
½ teaspoon salt
1½ cups instant potato flakes
  3 ounces PHILADELPHIA® Cream Cheese, cubed
  2 KRAFT® Singles

1. Heat oven to 375°F. Mix meat, barbecue sauce, bread crumbs and egg. Shape into loaf in 12×8-inch baking dish.

2. Bake 55 minutes. Meanwhile, bring water to boil in medium saucepan. Add milk, butter and salt; stir in potato flakes. Add cream cheese; stir until completely melted.

3. Spread potato mixture over meatloaf; top with Singles. Bake an additional 5 minutes or until Singles begin to melt.   *Makes 4 servings*

Round Out the Meal: Serve with a steamed green vegetable, such as green beans, and a whole wheat roll.

Great Substitute: Substitute 1 package (16 ounces) frozen LOUIS RICH® Ground Turkey for the ground beef.

Special Extra: Garnish with chopped fresh chives just before serving.

Cheesy Tuna Pie

2 cups cooked rice

2 cans (6 ounces each) tuna, drained and flaked

1 cup mayonnaise

1 cup (4 ounces) shredded Cheddar cheese

½ cup thinly sliced celery

½ cup sour cream

1 can (4 ounces) sliced black olives

2 tablespoons dried minced onion

1 refrigerated pie crust dough (½ of a 15-ounce package)

1. Preheat oven to 350°F. Spray 9-inch deep-dish pie pan with nonstick cooking spray.

2. Combine all ingredients except pie crust in medium bowl; mix well. Spoon into prepared pan. Top with pie crust; press edge to pan to seal. Cut slits for steam to escape.

3. Bake 20 minutes or until crust is browned and filling is bubbly.

Makes 6 servings

Chicken Broccoli Rice Casserole

3 cups cooked long-grain rice

4 boneless skinless chicken breasts (about 1 pound), cooked and cut into bite-size pieces

1½ pounds broccoli, cut into bite-size pieces and steamed until tender

2 cans (10¾ ounces each) condensed cream of celery soup, undiluted

¾ cup mayonnaise

½ cup whole milk

2 teaspoons curry powder

3 cups (12 ounces) shredded sharp Cheddar cheese

1. Preheat oven to 350°F. Grease 13×9-inch baking dish.

2. Spread cooked rice evenly in prepared dish. Top with chicken and broccoli. Mix soup, mayonnaise, milk and curry powder in medium bowl; pour over chicken and broccoli. Top with cheese.

3. Cover loosely with foil. Bake 45 minutes or until cheese melts and casserole is heated through.

Makes 4 to 6 servings

Tuscan-Style Sausage Skillet

  2 teaspoons olive oil
½ cup chopped fresh fennel
½ cup chopped sweet or yellow onion
  3 cloves garlic, minced
  1 can (about 14 ounces) fire-roasted diced tomatoes
  1 package (9 ounces) fully cooked chicken or turkey Italian sausage, cut into ½-inch pieces
¾ teaspoon dried rosemary
  1 can (about 15 ounces) navy or Great Northern beans, rinsed and drained
  4 cups baby spinach or torn spinach

1. Heat oil in large deep skillet over medium-high heat. Add fennel, onion and garlic; cook and stir 5 minutes.

2. Add tomatoes, sausage and rosemary to skillet. Reduce heat to low. Cover; simmer 10 minutes or until vegetables are tender. Stir in beans; cook over medium-high heat until heated through.

3. Add spinach to skillet. Cover; cook 2 minutes or until spinach wilts.

Makes 4 servings

Country Turkey Casserole

  1 can (10¾ ounces) CAMPBELL'S® Condensed Cream of Celery Soup (Regular or 98% Fat Free)
  1 can (10¾ ounces) CAMPBELL'S® Condensed Cream of Potato Soup
  1 cup milk
¼ teaspoon dried thyme leaves, crushed
⅛ teaspoon ground black pepper
  4 cups cooked cut-up vegetables*
  2 cups cubed cooked turkey or chicken
  4 cups prepared PEPPERIDGE FARM® Herb Seasoned Stuffing

Use a combination of cut green beans and sliced carrots.

1. Stir the soups, milk, thyme, black pepper, vegetables and turkey in a 3-quart shallow baking dish. Spoon the stuffing over the turkey mixture.

2. Bake at 400°F. for 25 minutes or until the stuffing is golden brown.

Makes 5 servings

Tuscan-Style Sausage Skillet

Ham Asparagus Gratin

　1 can (10¾ ounces) CAMPBELL'S® Condensed Cream of Asparagus Soup
　½ cup milk
　¼ teaspoon onion powder
　¼ teaspoon ground black pepper
　1½ cups cooked cut asparagus
　1½ cups cubed cooked ham
　2¼ cups corkscrew-shaped pasta (rotini), cooked and drained
　1 cup shredded Cheddar cheese or Swiss cheese

1. Stir the soup, milk, onion powder, black pepper, asparagus, ham, pasta and ½ cup cheese in a 2-quart shallow baking dish.

2. Bake at 400°F. for 25 minutes or until the ham mixture is hot and bubbling. Stir the ham mixture. Sprinkle with the remaining cheese.

3. Bake for 5 minutes or until the cheese is melted.　　*Makes 4 servings*

Barbecue Chicken with Corn Bread Topper

　1½ pounds boneless skinless chicken breasts and thighs, cut into ¾-inch cubes
　1 can (about 15 ounces) red beans, rinsed and drained
　1 can (8 ounces) tomato sauce
　1 cup chopped green bell pepper
　½ cup barbecue sauce
　1 package (6 ounces) corn bread mix, plus ingredients to prepare mix

1. Preheat oven to 375°F. Heat nonstick skillet over medium heat. Add chicken; cook and stir 5 minutes or until cooked through.

2. Combine chicken, beans, tomato sauce, bell pepper and barbecue sauce in microwavable 8-inch baking dish.

3. Loosely cover chicken mixture with plastic wrap or waxed paper. Microwave on MEDIUM-HIGH (70%) 8 minutes or until heated through, stirring after 4 minutes.

4. Meanwhile, prepare corn bread mix according to package directions. Spoon batter over chicken mixture. Bake 15 to 18 minutes or until toothpick inserted into center of corn bread layer comes out clean.

Makes 8 servings

Ham Asparagus Gratin

Biscuit-Topped Hearty Steak Pie

1½ pounds top round steak, cooked and cut into 1-inch cubes
1 package (9 ounces) frozen baby carrots
1 package (9 ounces) frozen peas and pearl onions
1 large baking potato, baked and cut into ½-inch pieces
1 jar (18 ounces) homestyle brown gravy
½ teaspoon dried thyme
½ teaspoon black pepper
1 can (10 ounces) refrigerated flaky buttermilk biscuit dough

1. Preheat oven to 375°F. Spray 2-quart casserole with nonstick cooking spray.

2. Combine steak, carrots, peas, potato, gravy, thyme and pepper in large bowl. Pour into prepared casserole.

3. Bake, uncovered, 40 minutes. Remove from oven. *Increase oven temperature to 400°F.* Top with biscuits and bake 8 to 10 minutes or until biscuits are golden brown.   *Makes 6 servings*

Variations: This casserole can be prepared with leftovers of almost any kind. Other steaks, roast beef, stew meat, pork, lamb or chicken can be substituted for the round steak. Adjust the gravy flavor to complement the meat. Red potatoes can be used in place of the baking potato. Choose your favorite vegetable combination, such as broccoli, cauliflower and carrots, or broccoli, corn and red peppers, as a substitute for the carrots, peas and onions.

Turkey & Green Bean Casserole

¼ **cup slivered almonds**

 1 **package (7 ounces) herb-seasoned stuffing cubes**

¾ **cup chicken broth**

 1 **can (about 10¾ ounces) condensed cream of mushroom soup, undiluted**

¼ **cup milk or half-and-half**

¼ **teaspoon black pepper**

 1 **package (10 ounces) frozen French-style green beans, thawed and drained**

 2 **cups cubed cooked turkey or chicken**

1. Preheat oven to 350°F. Spray 11×7-inch baking dish with nonstick cooking spray.

2. Spread almonds in single layer on baking sheet. Bake 5 minutes or until golden brown, stirring frequently.

3. Spread stuffing cubes in prepared dish. Drizzle with broth; stir to coat bread cubes with broth.

4. Combine soup, milk and pepper in large bowl. Add green beans and turkey; stir until blended. Spoon over stuffing cubes; top with almonds. Bake, uncovered, 30 to 35 minutes or until heated through.

Makes 4 servings

Enter his gates with thanksgiving, and his courts
with praise. Give thanks to him, bless his name.
Psalm 100:4 NRSV

Potato Sausage Casserole

1 pound bulk pork sausage or ground pork
1 can (10¾ ounces) condensed cream of mushroom soup, undiluted
¾ cup milk
½ cup chopped onion
½ teaspoon salt
¼ teaspoon black pepper
3 cups sliced potatoes
1 tablespoon butter, cut into small pieces
1½ cups (6 ounces) shredded Cheddar cheese
   Sliced green onions (optional)

1. Preheat oven to 350°F. Lightly spray 1½-quart casserole with nonstick cooking spray.

2. Brown sausage in large skillet over medium heat 6 to 8 minutes, stirring to break up meat. Drain fat.

3. Stir soup, milk, onion, salt and pepper in medium bowl.

4. Place half of potatoes in prepared casserole. Top with half of soup mixture; top with half of sausage. Repeat layers, ending with sausage. Dot with butter; cover with foil.

5. Bake 1¼ to 1½ hours or until potatoes are tender. Uncover casserole; sprinkle with cheese. Bake until cheese is melted and casserole is bubbly. Garnish with green onions.   *Makes 6 servings*

To prepare green onions, wash them thoroughly and trim off the roots. Remove any wilted or discolored layers. Green onions may be sliced, chopped, cut into lengths or used whole. The green tops can be cooked, but they cook more quickly than the white bases.

Fruited Corn Pudding

    5 cups thawed frozen corn, divided
    5 eggs
    ½ cup milk
 1½ cups whipping cream
    ⅓ cup unsalted butter, melted and cooled
    1 teaspoon vanilla
    ½ teaspoon salt
    ¼ teaspoon ground nutmeg
    3 tablespoons finely chopped dried apricots
    3 tablespoons dried cranberries or raisins
    3 tablespoons finely chopped dates
    2 tablespoons finely chopped dried pears or other dried fruit

1. Preheat oven to 350°F. Grease 13×9-inch baking dish.

2. Combine 3½ cups corn, eggs and milk in food processor; process until almost smooth.

3. Transfer corn mixture to large bowl. Add cream, butter, vanilla, salt and nutmeg; stir until well blended. Add remaining 1½ cups corn, apricots, cranberries, dates and pears; mix well. Pour mixture into prepared baking dish.

4. Bake 50 to 60 minutes or until center is set and top begins to brown. Let stand 10 to 15 minutes before serving.   *Makes 8 servings*

Mushroom Sage Stuffing

¼ cup (½ stick) butter
2 cups sliced shiitake mushroom caps
1 small onion, chopped
1 stalk celery, trimmed, chopped
2 teaspoons minced fresh sage
1 teaspoon grated orange peel
¼ teaspoon salt
¼ teaspoon black pepper
6 cups ½-inch cubes French or sourdough bread, toasted
1 cup chicken or vegetable broth

1. Preheat oven to 325°F. Grease shallow 2-quart casserole.

2. Melt butter in large saucepan or Dutch oven over medium-high heat. Add mushrooms, onion and celery; cook and stir 5 minutes or until vegetables are tender. Stir in sage, orange peel, salt and pepper. Stir in bread. Gradually add broth, stirring constantly to moisten bread.

3. Spoon into prepared casserole. Bake 30 minutes or until heated through and lightly browned.   *Makes 8 servings*

Scalloped Garlic Potatoes

3 medium all-purpose potatoes, peeled and thinly sliced (about 1½ pounds)
1 envelope LIPTON® RECIPE SECRETS® Savory Herb with Garlic Soup Mix
1 cup (½ pint) whipping or heavy cream
½ cup water

1. Preheat oven to 375°F. In lightly greased 2-quart shallow baking dish, arrange potatoes. In medium bowl, blend remaining ingredients; pour over potatoes.

2. Bake, uncovered, 45 minutes or until potatoes are tender.

Makes 4 servings

Asparagus with No-Cook Creamy Mustard Sauce

½ cup plain yogurt

2 tablespoons mayonnaise

1 tablespoon Dijon mustard

2 teaspoons lemon juice

½ teaspoon salt

2 cups water

1½ pounds asparagus spears, trimmed

⅛ teaspoon black pepper (optional)

1. For sauce, whisk yogurt, mayonnaise, mustard, lemon juice and salt in small bowl until smooth; set aside.

2. Bring water to a boil in large skillet over high heat. Add asparagus; return to a boil. Reduce heat; cover and simmer 3 minutes or until crisp-tender. Drain.

3. Place asparagus on serving platter; top with sauce. Sprinkle with pepper, if desired. *Makes 6 servings*

Choose fresh-looking asparagus stalks with closed, compact tips. Open tips are a sign of over-maturity. At home, keep asparagus in the refrigerator. Use it quickly to enjoy the best fresh flavor and texture.

New Potatoes and Peas

9 small new potatoes, cut into quarters (about 1½ pounds)
1 can (10¾ ounces) CAMPBELL'S® Condensed Cream of Mushroom Soup (Regular or 98% Fat Free)
⅓ cup milk
½ teaspoon dried thyme leaves or dill weed, crushed
⅛ teaspoon ground black pepper
1 package (10 ounces) frozen peas or peas with pearl onions, thawed and drained

1. Place the potatoes in a 4-quart saucepan. Cover the potatoes with water. Heat over high heat to a boil. Reduce the heat to medium. Cook for 8 minutes or until the potatoes are fork-tender. Drain the potatoes in a colander.

2. In the same saucepan, stir the soup, milk, thyme and black pepper. Stir in the potatoes and peas. Heat over low heat, stirring occasionally until heated through. *Makes 7 servings*

Savory Beets

2 tablespoons chopped onion
1 tablespoon butter
3 tablespoons honey
2 tablespoons red or white wine vinegar
⅛ teaspoon ground cloves
   Salt
1 can (16 ounces) sliced beets, drained

1. Cook and stir onion in butter in large skillet over medium heat until softened.

2. Add honey, vinegar, cloves and salt; cook and stir until mixture begins to boil. Add beets; cook until heated through. *Makes 4 servings*

Kentucky Cornbread & Sausage Stuffing

½ pound **BOB EVANS®** Original Recipe Roll Sausage
3 cups fresh bread cubes, dried or toasted
3 cups crumbled prepared cornbread
1 large apple, peeled and chopped
1 small onion, chopped
1 cup chicken or turkey broth
2 tablespoons minced fresh parsley
1 teaspoon salt
1 teaspoon rubbed sage or poultry seasoning
¼ teaspoon black pepper

Crumble sausage into small skillet. Cook over medium heat until browned, stirring occasionally. Place sausage and drippings in large bowl. Add remaining ingredients; toss lightly. Use to stuff chicken loosely just before roasting. Or, place stuffing in greased 13×9-inch baking dish. Add additional broth for moister stuffing, if desired. Bake in 350°F oven 30 minutes. Leftover stuffing should be removed from bird and stored separately in refrigerator. Reheat thoroughly before serving.

Makes enough stuffing for 5-pound chicken (8 side-dish servings)

Serving Suggestion: Double this recipe to stuff 12- to 15-pound turkey.

Green Beans with Pine Nuts

1 pound green beans, trimmed
2 tablespoons butter
2 tablespoons pine nuts
Salt and black pepper

1. Bring water to a boil in 3-quart saucepan. Add green beans; cook 6 to 8 minutes or until crisp-tender; drain.

2. Melt butter in large skillet over medium heat. Add pine nuts; cook, stirring frequently, until golden. Add beans; stir gently to coat beans with butter. Season with salt and pepper.

Makes 4 servings

Creamy Mashed Potato Bake

    3 cups mashed potatoes
    1 cup sour cream
    ¼ cup milk
    ¼ teaspoon garlic powder
    1⅓ cups FRENCH'S® French Fried Onions, divided
    1 cup (4 ounces) shredded Cheddar cheese, divided

1. Preheat oven to 350°F. Combine mashed potatoes, sour cream, milk and garlic powder.

2. Spoon half of mixture into 2-quart casserole. Sprinkle with ⅔ cup French Fried Onions and ½ cup cheese. Top with remaining potato mixture.

3. Bake 30 minutes or until hot. Top with remaining ⅔ cup onions and ½ cup cheese. Bake 5 minutes or until onions are golden.

Makes 6 servings

Classic Macaroni and Cheese

    3 tablespoons butter or margarine
    ¼ cup finely chopped onion (optional)
    2 tablespoons all-purpose flour
    ½ teaspoon salt
    ⅛ teaspoon black pepper
    2 cups milk
    2 cups (8 ounces) SARGENTO® Fancy Shredded Mild
        Cheddar Cheese, divided
    2 cups elbow macaroni, cooked and drained

Melt butter in medium saucepan over medium heat. Cook onion, if desired, in butter 5 minutes or until tender. Stir in flour, salt and pepper. Gradually add milk and cook, stirring occasionally, until thickened.

Remove from heat. Add 1½ cups cheese and stir until cheese is melted. Combine cheese sauce with cooked macaroni. Place in 1½-quart casserole; top with remaining cheese.

Bake in preheated 350°F oven 30 minutes or until bubbly and cheese is lightly browned.

Makes 6 servings

Crispy-Topped Creamy Spinach

2 packages (10 ounces each) frozen chopped spinach, thawed, well drained

1 container (8 ounces) PHILADELPHIA® Chive & Onion Cream Cheese Spread

½ cup KRAFT® Ranch Dressing

2 eggs, lightly beaten

1½ cups KRAFT® Shredded Cheddar Cheese, divided

1 cup crushed RITZ® Crackers, divided

HEAT oven to 375°F. Mix spinach, cream cheese spread, dressing, eggs and ¾ cup of the Cheddar cheese in large bowl. Stir in ½ cup of the crushed crackers.

SPOON spinach mixture evenly into greased 2-quart ovenproof casserole dish. Sprinkle with remaining ½ cup crushed crackers and remaining ¾ cup Cheddar cheese.

BAKE 20 to 25 minutes or until heated through and cheese on top is melted. *Makes 12 servings*

Healthy Living: Counting calories? Save 50 calories and 8 grams of fat per serving by using PHILADELPHIA® Chive & Onion Light Cream Cheese Spread, KRAFT® Light Ranch Dressing, KRAFT® 2% Milk Shredded Reduced Fat Cheddar Cheese and RITZ® Reduced Fat Crackers.

How to Thaw Frozen Spinach: Thaw frozen spinach in refrigerator overnight or unwrap, place in microwavable bowl and thaw in microwave as directed on package. Be sure to squeeze well after thawing to remove as much water as possible.

Country-Style Corn

4 slices bacon
1 tablespoon flour
1 can (about 15 ounces) corn, drained
1 can (about 15 ounces) cream-style corn
1 red bell pepper, diced
½ cup sliced green onions
Salt and black pepper

1. Cook bacon in large skillet over medium heat until crisp. Remove bacon and drain on paper towels. Crumble bacon; set aside.

2. Whisk flour into drippings in skillet. Add corn, cream-style corn and bell pepper; bring to a boil. Reduce heat to low; cook 10 minutes or until thickened.

3. Stir green onions and crumbled bacon into corn mixture. Season with salt and black pepper. *Makes 6 to 8 servings*

Balsamic Green Beans with Almonds

1 pound fresh green beans, trimmed
2 teaspoons olive oil
2 teaspoons balsamic vinegar
½ teaspoon salt
¼ teaspoon black pepper
2 tablespoons sliced almonds, toasted*

*Toast almonds in a dry skillet over medium heat 3 to 5 minutes or until fragrant, stirring frequently.

1. Place beans in medium saucepan; cover with water. Bring to a simmer over high heat. Reduce heat; simmer, uncovered, 4 to 8 minutes or until beans are crisp-tender. Drain well and return to saucepan.

2. Add oil, vinegar, salt and pepper; toss to coat. Sprinkle with almonds. *Makes 4 servings*

Hot Three-Bean Casserole

2 tablespoons olive oil

1 cup coarsely chopped onion

1 cup chopped celery

2 cloves garlic, minced

1 can (about 15 ounces) chickpeas, rinsed and drained

1 can (about 15 ounces) kidney beans, rinsed and drained

1 cup coarsely chopped tomato

1 cup water

1 can (about 8 ounces) tomato sauce

1 to 2 jalapeño peppers,* minced

1 tablespoon chili powder

2 teaspoons sugar

1½ teaspoons ground cumin

1 teaspoon salt

1 teaspoon dried oregano

¼ teaspoon black pepper

2½ cups (10 ounces) frozen cut green beans

Fresh oregano (optional)

Jalapeño peppers can sting and irritate the skin, so wear rubber gloves when handling peppers and do not touch your eyes.

1. Heat oil in large nonstick skillet over medium heat. Add onion, celery and garlic; cook and stir 5 minutes or until tender.

2. Add chickpeas, kidney beans, tomato, water, tomato sauce, jalapeño, chili powder, sugar, cumin, salt, dried oregano and black pepper; mix well. Bring to a boil. Reduce heat to low; simmer, uncovered, 20 minutes.

3. Add green beans; simmer 10 minutes or until tender. Garnish with fresh oregano.   *Makes 12 servings*

Chive & Onion Mashed Potatoes

2 pounds potatoes, peeled, quartered (about 6 cups)
½ cup milk
1 tub (8 ounces) PHILADELPHIA® Chive & Onion Cream
    Cheese Spread
¼ cup KRAFT® Ranch Dressing

1. Place potatoes and enough water to cover in 3-quart saucepan. Bring to a boil.

2. Reduce heat to medium; cook 20 to 25 minutes or until tender. Drain.

3. Mash potatoes, gradually stirring in milk, cream cheese spread and dressing until light and fluffy. Serve immediately.

Makes 10 servings (½ cup each)

Make Ahead: Mix ingredients as directed; spoon into 1½-quart casserole dish. Cover. Refrigerate several hours or overnight. When ready to serve, bake, uncovered, at 350°F 1 hour or until heated through.

Substitute: Substitute KRAFT® Three Cheese Ranch Dressing for Ranch Dressing.

For the best results, make sure that the potatoes are
fully cooked so they are soft enough to become
completely smooth.

Rice Pilaf with Dried Cherries and Almonds

½ cup slivered almonds
2 tablespoons butter
2 cups converted white rice
½ cup chopped onion
1 can (about 14 ounces) vegetable broth
1½ cups water
½ cup dried cherries

1. Cook and stir almonds in large nonstick skillet over medium heat until lightly browned. Remove from skillet; cool.

2. Melt butter in same skillet over low heat. Add rice and onion; cook and stir until rice is lightly browned. Add broth and water. Bring to a boil over high heat; reduce heat to low. Simmer, covered, 15 minutes.

3. Stir in almonds and cherries. Simmer 5 minutes or until liquid is absorbed and rice is tender. *Makes 12 servings*

Oven-Roasted Vegetables

1 envelope LIPTON® RECIPE SECRETS® Savory Herb with Garlic Soup Mix*
1½ pounds assorted fresh vegetables**
2 tablespoons olive oil

Also terrific with LIPTON® RECIPE SECRETS® Onion or Golden Onion Soup Mix.

**Use any combination of the following, sliced: zucchini; yellow squash; red, green or yellow bell peppers; carrots; celery or mushrooms.*

1. Preheat oven to 450°F. In large plastic bag or bowl, combine all ingredients. Close bag and shake, or toss in bowl, until vegetables are evenly coated.

2. In 13×9-inch baking or roasting pan, arrange vegetables; discard bag.

3. Bake uncovered, stirring once, 20 minutes or until vegetables are tender. *Makes 4 servings*

Tip: For a lower fat version, spray pan lightly with nonstick cooking spray and replace oil with 2 tablespoons water.

Rice Pilaf with Dried Cherries and Almonds

Broccoli & Cheese Casserole

1 can (10¾ ounces) CAMPBELL'S® Condensed Cream of Mushroom Soup (Regular or 98% Fat Free)

½ cup milk

2 teaspoons yellow mustard

1 bag (16 ounces) frozen broccoli flowerets, thawed

1 cup shredded Cheddar cheese (4 ounces)

⅓ cup dry bread crumbs

2 teaspoons butter, melted

1. Stir the soup, milk, mustard, broccoli and cheese in a 1½-quart casserole.

2. Stir the bread crumbs and butter in a small bowl. Sprinkle the crumb mixture over the broccoli mixture.

3. Bake at 350°F. for 30 minutes or until the mixture is hot and bubbling.

Makes 6 servings

Rice Is Nice: Add 2 cups cooked white rice to the broccoli mixture before baking.

Cheese Change-Up: Substitute mozzarella cheese for the Cheddar.

Glazed Carrots

1 tablespoon butter

1 package (16 ounces) baby carrots

¾ cup apple juice

2 teaspoons honey

1 teaspoon apple cider vinegar

Salt and pepper

1. Melt butter in medium skillet over medium-high heat. Add carrots; cook and stir 7 minutes or until just beginning to brown.

2. Add apple juice, honey and vinegar; bring to a boil. Reduce heat to medium; cook 15 minutes or until carrots are tender and glazed, stirring occasionally. Season with salt and pepper.

Makes 4 servings

Toasted Coconut-Pecan Sweet Potato Casserole

2 cans (15 ounces each) sweet potatoes in heavy syrup, drained
½ cup (1 stick) butter, softened
¼ cup packed light brown sugar
1 egg
½ teaspoon vanilla
⅛ teaspoon salt
½ cup chopped pecans
¼ cup flaked sweetened coconut
2 tablespoons golden raisins (optional)

1. Preheat oven to 325°F. Spray 8-inch square baking dish with nonstick cooking spray. Combine potatoes, butter, brown sugar, egg, vanilla and salt in food processor or blender; process until smooth.

2. Spoon potato mixture into prepared dish. Sprinkle evenly with pecans, coconut and raisins, if desired. Bake 22 to 25 minutes or until coconut is lightly golden. *Makes 4 servings*

Loaded Baked Potato Casserole

1 bag (32 ounces) Southern-style hash-brown potatoes, thawed (about 7½ cups)
1 can (6 ounces) FRENCH'S® French Fried Onions (2⅔ cups)
1 cup frozen peas, thawed
1 cup shredded Cheddar cheese (4 ounces)
4 slices bacon, cooked and crumbled
2 cans (10¾ ounces each) CAMPBELL'S® Condensed Cream of Celery Soup (Regular or 98% Fat Free)
1 cup milk

1. Stir the potatoes, 1⅓ cups of the onions, peas, cheese and bacon in a 13×9-inch (3-quart) shallow baking dish. Stir the soup and milk in a medium bowl. Pour the soup mixture over the potato mixture. Cover.

2. Bake at 350°F. for 30 minutes or until hot. Stir.

3. Sprinkle with the remaining onions. Bake for 5 minutes more or until the onions are golden brown. *Makes 8 servings*

Toasted Coconut-Pecan
Sweet Potato Casserole

Garden Vegetable Pasta Salad with Bacon

12 ounces uncooked rotini pasta
2 cups broccoli florets
1 can (about 14 ounces) diced tomatoes
2 medium carrots, diagonally sliced
2 stalks celery, sliced
10 medium mushrooms, thinly sliced
½ medium red onion, thinly sliced
½ pound bacon, crisp-cooked and crumbled
1 bottle (8 ounces) Italian or ranch salad dressing
½ cup (2 ounces) shredded Cheddar cheese
1 tablespoon dried parsley
2 teaspoons dried basil
¼ teaspoon black pepper

1. Cook pasta according to package directions. Drain and rinse under cold water until cool.

2. Combine broccoli, tomatoes, carrots, celery, mushrooms and onion in large bowl. Add pasta and bacon; toss lightly.

3. Add salad dressing, cheese, parsley, basil and pepper; stir to combine.

Makes 6 to 8 servings

Listen to me, and eat what is good, and your soul will delight in the richest of fare.   Isaiah 55:2 NIV

Grilled Potato Salad

1 envelope LIPTON® RECIPE SECRETS® Onion Soup Mix*

⅓ cup olive oil

2 tablespoons red wine vinegar

1 clove garlic, finely chopped

2 pounds small red or all-purpose potatoes, cut into 1-inch cubes

1 tablespoon chopped fresh basil leaves *or* 1 teaspoon dried basil leaves, crushed

Freshly ground black pepper

*Also terrific with LIPTON® RECIPE SECRETS® Onion Mushroom or Golden Onion Soup Mix.

1. In large bowl, blend soup mix, oil, vinegar and garlic; stir in potatoes.

2. Grease 30×18-inch sheet of heavy-duty aluminum foil; top with potato mixture. Wrap foil loosely around mixture, sealing edges airtight with double fold. Place on another sheet of 30×18-inch foil; seal edges airtight with double fold in opposite direction.

3. Grill, shaking package occasionally and turning package once, 40 minutes or until potatoes are tender. Spoon into serving bowl and toss with basil and pepper. Serve slightly warm or at room temperature. *Makes 4 servings*

Oven Method: Preheat oven to 450°F. Prepare foil packet as above. Place in large baking pan on bottom rack and bake, turning packet once, 40 minutes or until potatoes are tender. Toss and serve as above.

Country Time Macaroni Salad

½ cup uncooked regular or whole wheat elbow macaroni
3 tablespoons mayonnaise
2 tablespoons plain yogurt
2 teaspoons sweet pickle relish
¾ teaspoon dried dill weed
½ teaspoon yellow mustard
¼ teaspoon salt
½ cup peas
½ cup chopped green bell pepper
⅓ cup thinly sliced celery
4 ounces ham, cubed
¼ cup shredded Cheddar cheese

1. Cook pasta according to package directions. Drain and rinse under cold water until cool

2. Meanwhile, combine mayonnaise, yogurt, relish, dill, mustard and salt in small bowl. Stir until well blended; set aside.

3. Combine peas, bell pepper, celery and ham in large bowl. Add pasta and mayonnaise mixture; mix well. Stir in cheese. Serve immediately.

Makes 4 servings

Go and enjoy choice food and sweet drinks, and send some to those who have nothing prepared. . . . The joy of the Lord is your strength.   Nehemiah 8:10 NIV

Marinated Bean and Vegetable Salad

¼ **cup orange juice**
3 **tablespoons white wine vinegar**
1 **tablespoon vegetable oil**
2 **cloves garlic, minced**
1 **can (about 15 ounces) Great Northern beans, rinsed and drained**
1 **can (about 15 ounces) kidney beans, rinsed and drained**
¼ **cup coarsely chopped red cabbage**
¼ **cup chopped red onion**
¼ **cup chopped green bell pepper**
¼ **cup chopped red bell pepper**
¼ **cup sliced celery**

1. Combine orange juice, vinegar, oil and garlic in small jar with lid; shake well.

2. Combine beans, cabbage, onion, bell peppers and celery in large bowl. Pour dressing over bean mixture; toss to coat.

3. Cover and refrigerate 1 to 2 hours to allow flavors to blend. Toss before serving.
Makes 8 servings

Dried beans are a great alternative to canned beans.
They are less expensive and have a firmer texture
and fresher flavor. Look for dried beans in plastic
packages or in bulk. They will keep up to one year in
your pantry. Make a large batch of beans and freeze
the leftovers to save future soaking and cooking time.

Tangy Rice, Apple and Cabbage Slaw

⅔ cup Celery Seed Vinaigrette (recipe follows)
2 cups water
2 teaspoons butter
¼ teaspoon salt
¾ cup uncooked long grain white rice
2 cups shredded red and green cabbage or prepared coleslaw mix
1½ cups chopped unpeeled tart red apples
½ cup chopped green onions
½ cup grated carrots
½ cup slivered almonds

1. Prepare Celery Seed Vinaigrette; set aside.

2. Bring water, butter and salt to a boil in medium saucepan over medium-high heat; stir in rice. Reduce heat to low; simmer, covered, 20 minutes. Remove from heat. Let stand 5 minutes or until water is absorbed.

3. Combine cabbage, apples, green onions, carrots and almonds in large bowl. Add rice; mix well.

4. Stir in Celery Seed Vinaigrette; toss until well combined. Cover and refrigerate until ready to serve.　　　　*Makes 6 to 8 servings*

Celery Seed Vinaigrette: Combine ½ cup vegetable oil, 3 tablespoons honey, 2 tablespoons white wine vinegar, 1 teaspoon celery seed and ¾ teaspoon dry mustard in small bowl; mix well. Season with salt. Cover and store in refrigerator. Whisk before using. Celery Seed Vinaigrette can be prepared up to 2 days ahead.

Minestrone Salad

1 can (about 15 ounces) chickpeas, rinsed and drained
1 large tomato, chopped
2 stalks celery, chopped
1 cup cooked macaroni
¼ cup shredded Parmesan cheese
2 tablespoons Italian dressing
  Salt and black pepper

Combine chickpeas, tomato, celery, macaroni, Parmesan cheese and dressing in large bowl; mix well. Season with salt and pepper.

Makes 4 servings

Picnic Potato Salad

 2 pounds red potatoes
⅓ cup mayonnaise
⅓ cup sour cream
 2 to 3 tablespoons spicy brown or whole grain mustard
¾ teaspoon salt
¼ teaspoon black pepper
 2 hard-cooked eggs, peeled and chopped
½ cup crumbled, crisp-cooked bacon, plus additional for garnish
¼ cup chopped fresh chives (optional)

1. Place potatoes in large saucepan; cover with water. Bring to a boil over high heat. Reduce heat to low; simmer, covered, 20 to 25 minutes or until tender. Drain and rinse under cold water until cool.

2. Meanwhile, combine mayonnaise, sour cream, mustard, salt and pepper in large bowl; mix well.

3. Peel potatoes, if desired. Cut into chunks; add to mayonnaise mixture. Add eggs, bacon and chives, if desired; mix gently. Cover and refrigerate at least 2 hours or up to 24 hours. Garnish with additional bacon just before serving.

Makes 8 to 10 servings

Minestrone Salad

Crunchy Onion Layered Salad with Dilly Dijon Dressing

Layered Salad
4 cups washed and torn salad greens

8 ounces boiled ham, cut into cubes

4 hard-cooked eggs, chopped

2 ripe tomatoes, chopped

1 bell pepper (green, red or yellow), seeded and chopped

1 bunch radishes, sliced

1 package (9 ounces) frozen peas, thawed and drained

1⅓ cups FRENCH'S® French Fried Onions

Dilly Dijon Dressing
1 cup regular or reduced-fat mayonnaise

1 cup buttermilk or whole milk

¼ cup FRENCH'S® Honey Dijon Mustard

1 package (1 ounce) ranch salad dressing mix

½ teaspoon dried dill weed

Layer salad ingredients in 3-quart straight-sided glass bowl. Combine Dilly Dijon Dressing ingredients in small bowl; mix well. Spoon over salad just before serving. Garnish as desired.

Makes 4 main-dish or 6 side-dish servings (about 2 cups dressing)

Tip: For extra-crispy flavor, place French Fried Onions on a microwave-safe plate. Microwave on HIGH 1 to 2 minutes until golden.

Caribbean Black Bean and Rice Salad

2 cups cooked rice, cooled
1 can (about 15 ounces) black beans, rinsed and drained
1 cup chopped red bell pepper
½ cup halved and thinly sliced radishes
½ cup matchstick carrots
¼ cup lime juice
¼ cup extra virgin olive oil
¼ cup chopped cilantro
1 clove garlic, minced
1 teaspoon grated lime peel
1 teaspoon salt
¼ teaspoon black pepper
⅛ teaspoon dried red pepper flakes

1. Combine rice, beans, bell pepper, radishes and carrots in large bowl.

2. Whisk lime juice, olive oil, cilantro, garlic, lime peel, salt, black pepper and red pepper flakes in small bowl. Stir into salad; serve immediately.

Makes 6 servings

Tip: To make the salad in advance, combine all ingredients except lime juice and oil; cover and refrigerate. Stir in lime juice and oil just before serving.

Thanksgiving is nothing if not a glad and reverent
lifting of the heart to God in honour and praise
for His goodness.   James R. Miller

Carrot Raisin Salad

2 to 3 carrots, shredded* (1½ cups)
¼ cup raisins
¼ cup canned crushed pineapple, drained
1 tablespoon plain yogurt
4 lettuce leaves (optional)

Shredded carrots are available in the produce section of the supermarket, but this recipe is better with freshly shredded carrots.

1. Combine carrots, raisins, pineapple and yogurt in large bowl.

2. Cover and refrigerate 2 hours; stir occasionally. Serve on lettuce leaves, if desired. *Makes 4 servings*

Marinated Tomato Salad

2 cups cherry tomatoes, cut into halves
1 large cucumber, cut in half lengthwise and sliced
1 large yellow or red bell pepper, cut into strips
3 slices red onion, quartered
2 tablespoons balsamic vinegar
1 tablespoon olive oil
½ teaspoon dried basil
¼ teaspoon onion salt
¼ teaspoon garlic powder
¼ teaspoon dried oregano

1. Combine tomatoes, cucumber, bell pepper and onion in large bowl.

2. Whisk vinegar, oil, basil, onion salt, garlic powder and oregano in small bowl. Pour over vegetables; mix well. Serve immediately or cover and refrigerate 2 hours for flavors to blend. *Makes 6 to 8 servings*

Carrot Raisin Salad

Green Bean and Egg Salad

1 pound green beans, trimmed and cut into 2-inch pieces
3 hard-cooked eggs, peeled and chopped
2 stalks celery, sliced
½ cup Cheddar cheese cubes (¼-inch cubes)
¼ cup chopped red onion
⅓ cup mayonnaise
2 teaspoons cider vinegar
1½ teaspoons sugar
½ teaspoon salt
½ teaspoon celery seed
⅛ teaspoon black pepper

1. Bring large saucepan of water to a boil; cook beans 8 to 10 minutes or until tender. Drain and rinse under cold water until cool.

2. Combine beans, eggs, celery, cheese and onion in large bowl. Combine mayonnaise, vinegar, sugar, salt, celery seed and pepper in small bowl; mix well. Add to bean mixture; mix gently.

3. Cover and refrigerate at least 1 hour before serving.

Makes 6 servings

To prepare hard-cooked eggs, place the eggs in a single layer in a saucepan. Add cold water to cover the eggs by 1 inch; cover and bring to a boil over high heat. Remove the pan from the heat and let stand 15 minutes. Immediately pour off the water, cover the eggs with cold water and let stand until the eggs have cooled.

Green Bean and Egg Salad

Santa Fe Salad

2 cups cooked brown rice, cooled
1 can (about 15 ounces) black beans or pinto beans, rinsed
and drained
1 can (15 ounces) whole kernel corn, drained
¼ cup minced onion
¼ cup white vinegar
2 tablespoons chopped cilantro
2 tablespoons vegetable oil
2 jalapeño peppers,* minced
2 teaspoons chili powder
1 teaspoon salt

Jalapeño peppers can sting and irritate the skin, so wear rubber gloves when handling peppers and do not touch your eyes.

1. Combine rice, beans, corn and onion in medium bowl.

2. Combine vinegar, cilantro, oil, jalapeños, chili powder and salt in small jar with lid; shake well. Pour over rice mixture; toss lightly. Cover and refrigerate 2 to 3 hours to allow flavors to blend. Stir before serving.

Makes 6 servings

Cilantro is a fresh leafy herb that looks a lot like Italian parsley. Its distinctive flavor complements spicy foods, especially Mexican, Caribbean, Thai and Vietnamese dishes.

Summertime Fruit Medley

2 large ripe peaches, peeled and sliced
2 large ripe nectarines, sliced
1 large ripe mango, peeled and cut into 1-inch chunks
1 cup blueberries
2 cups orange juice
¼ cup amaretto *or* ½ teaspoon almond extract
2 tablespoons sugar
   Fresh mint (optional)

1. Combine peaches, nectarines, mango and blueberries in large bowl.

2. Whisk orange juice, amaretto and sugar in small bowl until sugar is dissolved. Pour over fruit mixture; toss to coat. Marinate 1 hour at room temperature, gently stirring occasionally. Garnish with fresh mint.

Makes 8 servings

Mangoes have a large central seed that clings tenaciously to the flesh. Do not try to cut the mango in half and twist the two halves apart, as is often directed. To prepare a mango, hold it, stem end up, on a cutting board. Using a utility knife, make a vertical cut on the flat side of the mango from the top to the bottom about ½ inch to the right of the stem and seed. Repeat on the opposite flat side of the mango.

Chilled Lemonade Desserts

3 cups boiling water
2 packages (4-serving size each) JELL-O® Lemon Flavor Gelatin
1 package (8 ounces) PHILADELPHIA® Cream Cheese, softened
1 can (6 ounces) frozen lemonade concentrate, thawed
1 tub (8 ounces) COOL WHIP® Whipped Topping, thawed
   Raspberries, blueberries and lemon slices, optional

STIR boiling water into dry gelatin mixes in large bowl at least 2 minutes until completely dissolved; set aside. Beat cream cheese and lemonade concentrate in large bowl with electric mixer on low speed until well blended. Add gelatin; mix well. Refrigerate 2 hours or until thickened (spoon drawn through leaves definite impression).

ADD whipped topping; stir with wire whisk until well blended. Pour evenly into 14 small dessert dishes.

REFRIGERATE 4 hours or until firm. Garnish with berries and lemon slices just before serving, if desired. Store leftover desserts in refrigerator.

Makes 14 servings (½ cup each)

Variation: Prepare as directed, using JELL-O® Strawberry Flavor Gelatin. Garnish with sliced fresh strawberries, if desired.

There is nothing better for people under the sun
than to eat, and drink, and enjoy themselves.
Ecclesiastes 8:15 NRSV

Ambrosia

1 can (20 ounces) DOLE® Pineapple Chunks, drained or
    2 cups DOLE® Frozen Tropical Gold Pineapple Chunks,
    partially thawed
1 can (11 or 15 ounces) DOLE® Mandarin Oranges, drained
1 DOLE® Banana, sliced
1½ cups seedless grapes
½ cup miniature marshmallows
1 cup vanilla low fat yogurt
¼ cup flaked coconut, toasted

• Combine pineapple chunks, mandarin oranges, banana, grapes and marshmallows in medium bowl.

• Stir yogurt into fruit mixture. Sprinkle with coconut.

Makes 4 to 6 servings

Honey Tea Cooler

1 pint fresh strawberries, stemmed
¼ cup honey
1 can (6 ounces) frozen orange juice concentrate
2 cups brewed green tea, cooled

1. Combine strawberries and honey in blender or food processor; blend until smooth.

2. Add orange juice concentrate; blend until smooth. Stir into cooled tea. Serve over ice.

Makes 4 servings

Ambrosia

Pineapple-Lemonade Pizzazz

   3 cups peach nectar, mango nectar, peach-mango juice or
      passion fruit juice, chilled
   3 cups pineapple juice, chilled
   1 can (12 ounces) frozen lemonade concentrate, thawed
 2½ cups club soda or sparkling water, chilled
   2 cups ginger ale, chilled
      Crushed ice

1. Combine peach nectar, pineapple juice and lemonade concentrate in 1-gallon pitcher.

2. Gently stir in club soda and ginger ale. Serve immediately over crushed ice. *Makes 16 (6-ounce) servings*

Cranberry Crunch Gelatin

   2 cups boiling water
   2 packages (4-serving size each) cherry-flavored gelatin
   1 can (16 ounces) whole berry cranberry sauce
 1½ cups miniature marshmallows
   1 cup coarsely chopped walnuts

1. Stir boiling water into gelatin in large bowl 2 minutes or until completely dissolved. Chill about 2 hours or until slightly set.

2. Fold cranberry sauce, marshmallows and walnuts into gelatin mixture. Pour into 6-cup gelatin mold. Cover and refrigerate at least 4 hours or until set. Remove from mold. *Makes 8 servings*

Strawberry-Orange Delight

2½ cups boiling water

  3 packages (4-serving size each) JELL-O® Strawberry Flavor Gelatin

2¾ cups cold water

  1 can (11 ounces) mandarin orange segments, drained

  4 ounces (½ of 8-ounce package) PHILADELPHIA® Cream Cheese, softened

  2 tablespoons sugar

  1 tub (8 ounces) COOL WHIP® Whipped Topping, thawed, divided

STIR boiling water into dry gelatin mixes in medium bowl at least 2 minutes until completely dissolved. Stir in cold water. Refrigerate about 1¼ hours or until slightly thickened (consistency of unbeaten egg whites). Reserve a few oranges for garnish. Gently stir remaining oranges into thickened gelatin. Set aside.

BEAT cream cheese and sugar in separate medium bowl with wire whisk until well blended. Gently stir in 2 cups of the whipped topping. Spoon into large serving bowl; cover with the gelatin mixture.

REFRIGERATE 2 hours or until firm. Top with the remaining whipped topping and reserved oranges just before serving.

Makes 16 servings (about ½ cup each)

How To Soften Cream Cheese: Place measured amount of cream cheese in microwavable bowl. Microwave on HIGH 10 seconds or until slightly softened.

Fresh Summer Fruit Fool

1 cup sliced peeled peaches (about 2 small)
1 cup sliced peeled plums (about 2 large)
1 cup fresh raspberries
8 tablespoons powdered sugar, divided
1 tablespoon fresh lime juice
1 cup whipping cream
   Grated lime peel (optional)

1. Place peaches, plums, raspberries, 6 tablespoons powdered sugar and lime juice in blender; blend until smooth. Cover and refrigerate at least 1 hour.

2. Beat cream in large bowl with electric mixer at high speed until soft peaks form. Add remaining 2 tablespoons powdered sugar; beat until stiff. Fold in fruit mixture. Spoon into serving bowl; garnish with lime peel.

Makes 4 servings

Variation: Mango is also excellent in this dessert. Peel and slice 1 medium mango and substitute for the peaches.

One medium lime will yield about 1½ tablespoons juice and 1½ teaspoons grated peel.

Fruit Pizza

1 package (20 ounces) refrigerated sliceable sugar cookies, sliced
1 package (8 ounces) PHILADELPHIA® Cream Cheese, softened
¼ cup sugar
½ teaspoon vanilla
   Assorted fruit, such as sliced kiwi, strawberries, blueberries
      and drained, canned mandarin orange segments
¼ cup apricot preserves, pressed through sieve to remove lumps
1 tablespoon water

HEAT oven to 375°F. Line 12-inch pizza pan with foil; spray with cooking spray. Arrange cookie dough slices in single layer in prepared pan; press together to form crust. Bake 14 minutes; cool. Invert onto serving plate; carefully remove foil. Invert onto large serving plate or tray so crust is right-side-up.

BEAT cream cheese, sugar and vanilla with electric mixer on medium speed until well blended. Spread over crust.

ARRANGE fruit over cream cheese layer. Mix preserves and water; brush over fruit. Refrigerate 2 hours. Cut into 12 wedges to serve. Store leftover dessert in refrigerator.   *Makes 12 servings (1 wedge each)*

*Jesus said to them, "I am the bread of life. Whoever
comes to me will never be hungry, and whoever
believes in me will never be thirsty."*
John 6:35 NRSV

Dried Fruit Compote

1 cup water
1 cup apple juice
½ cup Rhine wine or additional apple juice
¼ cup packed light brown sugar
2 cinnamon sticks
4 whole allspice berries
4 whole cloves
4 whole black peppercorns
1 package (8 ounces) dried mixed fruit

1. Combine water, apple juice, wine and brown sugar in medium saucepan.

2. Wrap cinnamon sticks, allspice berries, cloves and peppercorns in 8-inch square of double thickness cheesecloth. Tie securely with string. Add to saucepan; stir in fruit.

3. Bring to a boil over high heat. Reduce heat to low; cover and simmer 12 to 15 minutes or until fruit is tender, stirring once. Cool; discard cheesecloth bag and spices.

4. Serve compote warm, at room temperature or chilled.

Makes 6 servings

Note: This recipe can be prepared with ground spices instead of whole spices. Substitute ½ teaspoon ground cinnamon for cinnamon sticks, ¼ teaspoon ground allspice for allspice berries, ⅛ teaspoon ground cloves for whole cloves and ⅛ teaspoon freshly ground black pepper for peppercorns. Wrap in cheesecloth or add directly to saucepan. Proceed as directed.

Lime & Pineapple Seafoam Salad

2 cans (8 ounces each) crushed pineapple in juice
1 package (4-serving size) lime gelatin
1 cup boiling water
½ cup cold water
1 package (8 ounces) cream cheese, softened
¾ cup coarsely chopped pecans
⅔ cup celery slices
1½ cups thawed whipped topping

1. Drain pineapple well. Reserve 3 tablespoons juice.

2. Place gelatin in medium bowl; stir in boiling water at least 2 minutes until gelatin is dissolved. Stir in cold water and reserved 3 tablespoons pineapple juice.

3. Beat cream cheese in large bowl with electric mixer at medium speed until smooth. Beat in ¼ cup gelatin mixture until blended. Slowly beat in remaining gelatin mixture. Cover and refrigerate about 1 hour or until thick.

4. Stir in pineapple, pecans and celery. Fold in whipped topping. Pour into clear glass serving dish. Cover and refrigerate about 2 hours or until set.

Makes 8 to 10 servings

Summer Berry Trifle

1 cup boiling water
1 package (6 ounces) JELL-O® Strawberry Flavor Gelatin
   Ice cubes
½ cup cold water
2 cups mixed berries (raspberries, blueberries, strawberries)
1 package (8 ounces) PHILADELPHIA® Cream Cheese, softened
1¼ cups cold milk, divided
1 package (3.4 ounces) JELL-O® Cheesecake or Vanilla Flavor
   Instant Pudding
1 tub (6 ounces) COOL WHIP® DIPS Strawberry Creme, thawed
1 package (10.75 ounces) pound cake, cubed

STIR boiling water into dry gelatin in large bowl at least 2 minutes until completely dissolved. Add enough ice to cold water to measure 1 cup. Add to gelatin; stir until ice is completely melted. Let stand about 15 minutes or until thickened. (Spoon drawn through gelatin leaves definite impression.) Stir in berries.

PLACE cream cheese in large bowl; beat with wire whisk until creamy. Gradually add ¼ cup of the milk, beating until well blended. Add remaining 1 cup milk and dry pudding mix; beat 2 minutes or until well blended. Gently stir in COOL WHIP® DIPS. Set aside.

PLACE about half of the cake cubes in bottom of large serving bowl; cover with half of the pudding mixture. Top with layers of the gelatin mixture, remaining cake cubes and remaining pudding mixture. Refrigerate at least 1 hour or until ready to serve. Store leftover dessert in refrigerator.

Makes 18 servings

Jazz It Up: Garnish with additional berries just before serving.

Variation: Prepare as directed, using JELL-O® Brand Strawberry Flavor Sugar Free Low Calorie Gelatin, COOL WHIP® LITE Whipped Topping and reduced fat or fat free pound cake.

Cranberry-Pineapple Punch

2½ cups cranberry juice, chilled
2 cups pineapple juice, chilled
½ teaspoon almond extract
2½ cups ginger ale, chilled
Ice cubes

Combine cranberry juice, pineapple juice and almond extract in large pitcher. Gently stir in ginger ale. Serve over ice cubes.

Makes about 9 (6-ounce) servings

Watergate Salad

1 package (4-serving size) instant pistachio pudding
   and pie filling
1 can (20 ounces) DOLE® Crushed Pineapple, undrained
1 cup miniature marshmallows
½ cup chopped pecans
1½ cups (½ of 8-ounces tub) thawed whipped topping

• Mix dry pudding mix, pineapple, marshmallows and pecans in large bowl until well blended. Gently stir in whipped topping; cover.

• Refrigerate 1 hour or until ready to serve.   *Makes 8 servings*

We shall take part in the feasts of the angel by contemplating not only the angels, but also, together, God Himself.   Saint Thomas Aquinas

Fruit 'n Juice Squares

1½ cups boiling water
   1 package (8-serving size) or 2 packages (4-serving size each)
      JELL-O® Brand Strawberry or Cranberry Flavor Gelatin
   1 cup cold orange juice
      Ice cubes
   1 tub (8 ounces) COOL WHIP® Whipped Topping, thawed, divided
   1 can (8¾ ounces) fruit cocktail, drained

STIR boiling water into gelatin in large bowl at least 2 minutes until completely dissolved. Mix cold juice and ice cubes to make 1¼ cups. Add to gelatin, stirring until slightly thickened (consistency of unbeaten egg whites). Remove any remaining ice. Refrigerate 45 minutes.

RESERVE 1 cup gelatin; set aside. Stir ½ of the whipped topping into remaining gelatin until smooth. Pour mixture into 8-inch square pan. Refrigerate about 5 minutes until set but not firm (should stick to finger when touched and should mound). Stir fruit into reserved gelatin and carefully spoon over creamy layer in pan.

REFRIGERATE 3 hours or until firm. Cut into squares and garnish with remaining whipped topping.   *Makes 9 servings*

Storage Know How: Keep gelatin refrigerated until ready to serve.

Great Substitute: 1 cup seasonal fresh berries may be substituted for canned fruit.

Raisin Apple Bread Pudding

- 4 cups white bread cubes
- 1 medium apple, chopped
- 1 cup raisins
- 2 large eggs
- 1 can (12 fluid ounces) NESTLÉ® CARNATION® Evaporated Milk
- ½ cup apple juice
- ½ cup granulated sugar
- 1½ teaspoons ground cinnamon
- 1 jar caramel ice cream topping (optional)

PREHEAT oven to 350°F. Grease 11×7-inch baking dish.

COMBINE bread, apple and raisins in large bowl. Beat eggs in medium bowl. Stir in evaporated milk, apple juice, sugar and cinnamon; mix well. Pour egg mixture over bread mixture, pressing bread into milk mixture; let stand for 10 minutes. Pour into prepared baking dish.

BAKE for 40 to 45 minutes or until set and apples are tender. Serve warm with caramel topping. *Makes 8 servings*

Always use the type of bread called for in the recipe.
Substituting a different bread can affect the amount
of liquid that is absorbed. The pudding is done when a
knife inserted in the center comes out clean.

Chunky Nut Blondie Drops

1¼ cups packed light brown sugar

1 cup (2 sticks) butter, softened

½ cup granulated sugar

2 eggs

1½ teaspoons vanilla

2½ cups all-purpose flour

1 teaspoon baking powder

½ teaspoon salt

¼ teaspoon baking soda

1½ cups coarsely chopped chocolate squares or nuggets
   with truffle or caramel centers

1¼ cups coarsely chopped pecans, toasted*

1¼ cups coarsely chopped walnuts, toasted*

To toast nuts, spread in single layer on cookie sheet. Bake in preheated 350°F oven 8 to 10 minutes or until golden brown, stirring frequently.

1. Preheat oven to 350°F. Line cookie sheets with parchment paper.

2. Beat brown sugar, butter and granulated sugar in large bowl with electric mixer at medium speed until well blended. Add eggs and vanilla; beat until well blended. Combine flour, baking powder, salt and baking soda in small bowl; gradually add to butter mixture, beating after each addition. Stir in chocolate and nuts.

3. Drop dough by rounded tablespoonfuls about 1½ inches apart onto prepared cookie sheets. (If dough is too soft, refrigerate about 1 hour before baking.)

4. Bake 15 to 17 minutes or until golden brown. Cool on cookie sheets 2 minutes. Remove to wire racks; cool completely.

Makes about 4 dozen cookies

Strawberry-Swirl Cake

- 1 package (2-layer size) white cake mix
- 1 package (4-serving size) JELL-O® Strawberry Flavor Gelatin
- ⅔ cup BREAKSTONE'S® or KNUDSEN® Sour Cream
- ⅔ cup powdered sugar
- 1 tub (8 ounces) COOL WHIP® Whipped Topping, thawed
- 1 cup sliced strawberries, plus 2 whole strawberries for garnish

PREHEAT oven to 350°F. Grease 2 (8- or 9-inch) round cake pans; set aside. Prepare cake batter as directed on package. Pour half of the batter into medium bowl. Add dry gelatin mix; stir until well blended. Spoon half of the white batter and half of the pink batter, side by side, into each prepared pan. Lightly swirl batters together using a teaspoon. (Do not overswirl, or the color of the cake will be all pink and not pink and white marbled.)

BAKE 30 minutes. Cool 30 minutes in pans. Remove to wire racks; cool completely.

MIX sour cream and powdered sugar in medium bowl until well blended. Gently stir in whipped topping. Place 1 of the cake layers on serving plate; spread top with 1 cup of the whipped topping mixture. Top with 1 cup of the strawberries and remaining cake layer. Spread top and sides of cake with remaining whipped topping mixture. Garnish with whole strawberries just before serving. Store leftover cake in refrigerator.

Makes 16 servings (1 slice each)

How to Prevent Air Bubbles: To release any air bubbles from the cake batter, lightly tap cake pans on counter before baking. Any small air bubbles will rise to the surface.

Berry Berry Streusel Bars

1½ cups QUAKER® Oats (quick or old fashioned, uncooked)
1¼ cups all-purpose flour
 ½ cup firmly packed brown sugar
 ¾ cup (1½ sticks) butter or margarine, melted
 1 cup fresh or frozen blueberries (do not thaw)
 ⅓ cup raspberry or strawberry preserves
 1 teaspoon all-purpose flour
 ½ teaspoon grated lemon peel (optional)

1. Heat oven to 350°F. Combine oats, flour, brown sugar and butter; mix until crumbly. Reserve 1 cup oat mixture for topping. Set aside. Press remaining mixture onto bottom of ungreased 8- or 9-inch square baking pan. Bake 13 to 15 minutes or until light golden brown. Cool slightly.

2. Combine blueberries, preserves, flour and lemon peel, if desired, in medium bowl; mix gently. Spread over crust. Sprinkle with reserved oat mixture, patting gently.

3. Bake 20 to 22 minutes or until light golden brown. Cool completely. Cut into bars. Store tightly covered.　　　　*Makes 16 bars*

Lemony Pound Cake

 1 package (4-serving size) lemon-flavor gelatin
 ¾ cup boiling water
 1 package DUNCAN HINES® Moist Deluxe® Classic Yellow Cake Mix
 4 eggs
 ¾ cup vegetable oil
 1 can (6 ounces) frozen lemonade concentrate, thawed
 ½ cup granulated sugar

1. Preheat oven to 350°F. Grease and flour 10-inch tube pan.

2. Dissolve gelatin in water in large mixing bowl; cool. Stir in cake mix, eggs and oil. Beat at medium speed with electric mixer for 2 minutes. Spoon into prepared pan.

3. Bake 50 minutes or until toothpick inserted in center comes out clean. Mix lemonade concentrate and sugar in small bowl. Pour over hot cake; cool in pan 1 hour. Remove from pan. Cool completely.
　　　　Makes 12 to 16 servings

TOLL HOUSE® Crumbcake

Topping

- ⅓ cup packed brown sugar
- 2 tablespoons butter or margarine, softened
- 1 tablespoon all-purpose flour
- ½ cup chopped nuts
- 2 cups (12-ounce package) NESTLÉ® TOLL HOUSE® Semi-Sweet Chocolate Mini Morsels, divided

Cake

- 1¾ cups all-purpose flour
- 1 teaspoon baking powder
- 1 teaspoon baking soda
- ¼ teaspoon salt
- ¾ cup granulated sugar
- ½ cup (1 stick) butter or margarine, softened
- 1 teaspoon vanilla extract
- 3 large eggs
- 1 cup sour cream

PREHEAT oven to 350°F. Grease 13×9-inch baking pan.

For Topping

COMBINE brown sugar, butter and flour in small bowl with pastry blender or two knives until crumbly. Stir in nuts and ½ cup morsels.

For Cake

COMBINE flour, baking powder, baking soda and salt in small bowl. Beat granulated sugar, butter and vanilla extract in large mixer bowl until creamy. Add eggs, one at a time, beating well after each addition. Gradually add flour mixture alternately with sour cream. Fold in remaining 1½ cups morsels. Spread into prepared baking pan; sprinkle with topping.

BAKE for 25 to 35 minutes or until wooden pick inserted in center comes out clean. Cool in pan on wire rack. *Makes 12 servings*

Apple Toffee Crisp

    5 cups (about 5 medium apples) peeled and sliced
        Granny Smith apples
    5 cups (about 5 medium apples) peeled and sliced
        McIntosh apples
 1¼ cups sugar, divided
 1¼ cups all-purpose flour, divided
  ¾ cup (1½ sticks) butter or margarine, divided
 1⅓ cups (8-ounce package) HEATH® BITS 'O BRICKLE® Toffee Bits
    1 cup uncooked rolled oats
  ½ teaspoon ground cinnamon
  ¼ teaspoon baking powder
  ¼ teaspoon baking soda
  ¼ teaspoon salt
        Whipped topping or ice cream (optional)

1. Heat oven to 375°F. Grease 13×9×2-inch baking pan.

2. Toss apple slices, ¾ cup sugar and ¼ cup flour, coating apples evenly. Spread in bottom of prepared pan. Dot with ¼ cup (½ stick) butter.

3. Stir together toffee bits, oats, remaining ½ cup sugar, remaining 1 cup flour, cinnamon, baking powder, baking soda and salt. Melt remaining ½ cup (1 stick) butter; add to oat mixture, mixing until crumbs are formed. Sprinkle crumb mixture over apples.

4. Bake 45 to 50 minutes or until topping is lightly browned and apples are tender. Serve warm with whipped topping or ice cream, if desired. Cover; refrigerate leftovers.   *Makes 10 to 12 servings*

Crunch Peach Cobbler

⅓ cup plus 1 tablespoon granulated sugar, divided
1 tablespoon cornstarch
1 can (29 ounces) *or* 2 cans (16 ounces each) cling peach
    slices in juice, drained and ¾ cup juice reserved
½ teaspoon vanilla
2 cups all-purpose flour, divided
½ cup packed light brown sugar
⅓ cup old-fashioned or quick oats
¼ cup (½ stick) butter, melted
½ teaspoon ground cinnamon
½ teaspoon salt
½ cup shortening
4 to 5 tablespoons cold water
Whipped cream (optional)

1. Combine ⅓ cup granulated sugar and cornstarch in small saucepan. Slowly add reserved ¾ cup peach juice; mix well. Cook over low heat, stirring constantly, until thickened. Stir in vanilla. Set aside.

2. For crumb topping, combine ½ cup flour, brown sugar, oats, butter and cinnamon in small bowl; stir until mixture forms coarse crumbs. Set aside.

3. Preheat oven to 350°F. Combine remaining 1½ cups flour, remaining 1 tablespoon granulated sugar and salt in medium bowl. Cut in shortening with pastry blender or two knives until mixture forms pea-sized pieces. Sprinkle water, 1 tablespoon at a time, over flour mixture. Toss lightly with fork after each addition until mixture holds together. Press together to form ball.

4. Roll dough into 10-inch square, ⅛ inch thick. Fold dough in half, then in half again. Carefully place folded dough in center of 8-inch square baking dish. Unfold and press onto bottom and about 1 inch up sides of dish. Arrange peaches over crust. Pour peach sauce over peaches. Sprinkle with crumb topping.

5. Bake 45 minutes or until topping is golden brown. Serve warm or at room temperature with whipped cream, if desired.

Makes 6 to 8 servings

Fudgy Chocolate Brownies

1⅓ cups all-purpose flour
¼ teaspoon baking soda
¼ teaspoon salt
1⅔ cups granulated sugar
½ cup (1 stick) butter or margarine, melted
4 packets (1 ounce *each*) NESTLÉ® TOLL HOUSE® CHOCO BAKE®
   Pre-Melted Unsweetened Chocolate Flavor
2 large eggs
2 tablespoons water
1½ teaspoons vanilla extract
½ cup chopped nuts (optional)

PREHEAT oven to 350°F. Grease 13×9-inch baking pan.

COMBINE flour, baking soda and salt in small bowl. Stir sugar, butter, Choco Bake, eggs, water and vanilla extract vigorously in large bowl. Stir in flour mixture. Stir in nuts. Spread into prepared baking pan.

BAKE for 18 to 22 minutes or until wooden pick inserted in center comes out slightly sticky. Cool completely in pan on wire rack. Cut into bars.

Makes 2 dozen brownies

Dump Cake

1 can (20 ounces) crushed pineapple with juice, undrained
1 can (21 ounces) cherry pie filling
1 package DUNCAN HINES® Moist Deluxe® Classic Yellow Cake Mix
1 cup chopped pecans or walnuts
½ cup (1 stick) butter or margarine, cut into thin slices

1. Preheat oven to 350°F. Grease 13×9-inch pan.

2. Dump pineapple with juice into prepared pan. Spread evenly. Dump in pie filling. Spread evenly. Sprinkle cake mix evenly over cherry layer. Sprinkle pecans over cake mix. Dot with butter. Bake at 350°F for 50 minutes or until top is lightly browned. Serve warm or at room temperature.

Makes 12 to 16 servings

Tip: You can use DUNCAN HINES® Moist Deluxe® Pineapple Supreme Cake Mix in place of Moist Deluxe® Yellow Cake Mix.

Holiday Walnut Berry Bites

MAZOLA PURE® Cooking Spray
2½ **cups flour**
1 **cup cold margarine, cut into pieces**
½ **cup confectioners' sugar**
½ **teaspoon salt**
1⅓ **cups KARO® Light Corn Syrup or KARO® Lite Syrup**
4 **eggs**
1 **cup sugar**
3 **tablespoons butter, melted**
2 **cups fresh or thawed frozen cranberries, coarsely chopped**
1 **cup walnuts, chopped**
1 **cup white chocolate chips**

Preheat oven to 350°F. Spray 15×10×1-inch baking pan with cooking spray. In large bowl beat flour, margarine, confectioners' sugar and salt with electric mixer at medium speed until mixture resembles coarse crumbs; press firmly and evenly into pan. Bake 20 minutes or until golden brown.

In large bowl, beat corn syrup, eggs, sugar and butter until well blended. Stir in cranberries and walnuts.

Spread mixture evenly over hot crust. Sprinkle white chocolate chips over top. Bake 25 to 30 minutes or until set. Cool completely on wire rack before cutting into bars.   *Makes 4 dozen bars*

Glazed Applesauce Spice Cake

1 cup packed light brown sugar
¾ cup (1½ sticks) butter, softened
3 eggs
1½ teaspoons vanilla
2¼ cups all-purpose flour
2 teaspoons baking soda
2 teaspoons ground cinnamon
¾ teaspoon ground nutmeg
½ teaspoon ground ginger
¼ teaspoon salt
1½ cups unsweetened applesauce
½ cup milk
⅔ cup chopped walnuts
⅔ cup butterscotch chips
1 cup sifted powdered sugar
2 to 3 tablespoons apple juice concentrate

1. Preheat oven to 350°F. Grease and lightly flour 12-cup bundt pan or 10-inch tube pan.

2. Beat brown sugar and butter in large bowl with electric mixer at medium speed until light and fluffy. Beat in eggs and vanilla until well blended. Combine flour, baking soda, cinnamon, nutmeg, ginger and salt in medium bowl. Add flour mixture to butter mixture alternately with applesauce and milk, beginning and ending with flour mixture, beating well after each addition. Stir in walnuts and butterscotch chips. Pour into prepared pan.

3. Bake 45 to 50 minutes or until toothpick inserted near center comes out clean. Cool in pan 15 minutes. Remove to wire rack; cool completely.

4. Combine powdered sugar and apple juice concentrate in small bowl; stir to make stiff glaze. Spoon over top of cake. Store tightly covered at room temperature. *Makes about 12 servings*

Orange Marmalade Bars

Shortbread Crust
¼ cup hazelnuts, toasted, skins removed*
1 cup all-purpose flour
¼ cup packed brown sugar
6 tablespoons butter
1 egg
1 teaspoon vanilla

Filling
1 cup plus 2 teaspoons orange marmalade, divided
4 ounces cream cheese
¼ cup whipping cream
1 tablespoon granulated sugar
1 tablespoon grated orange peel
½ cup hazelnuts, toasted, skins removed and finely chopped*
2 tablespoons packed brown sugar
2 tablespoons melted butter
1 teaspoon all-purpose flour

Bake hazelnuts 5 minutes in a 300°F oven. Place nuts inside a towel and roll to remove skins.

1. Preheat oven to 375°F. Grease 13×9-inch baking pan.

2. For crust, process ¼ cup hazelnuts in food processor until finely chopped. Place in large bowl; whisk in flour and brown sugar. Cut in butter with pastry blender or two knives until mixture resembles coarse crumbs. Add egg and vanilla; stir just until dough forms.

3. Press dough evenly into prepared pan. Bake 12 to 15 minutes or until crust is golden brown. Spread 1 cup marmalade evenly over hot crust.

4. Beat cream cheese, cream, granulated sugar, remaining 2 teaspoons marmalade and orange peel in large bowl with electric mixer at low speed until smooth and creamy. Toss ½ cup finely chopped hazelnuts with brown sugar, butter and flour in small bowl until nuts are evenly coated; set aside.

5. Pour cream cheese mixture over marmalade and crust. Sprinkle hazelnut topping evenly over filling.

6. Bake 12 to 15 minutes or until topping is lightly browned and filling bubbles slightly. Cool 2 hours on wire rack. Cut into 2-inch bars.

Makes 2 dozen bars

Milk Chocolate Oatmeal Cookies

1¼ cups all-purpose flour
½ teaspoon baking powder
½ teaspoon baking soda
½ teaspoon ground cinnamon
¼ teaspoon salt
¾ cup (1½ sticks) butter or margarine, softened
¾ cup packed brown sugar
⅓ cup granulated sugar
1½ teaspoons vanilla extract
1 large egg
2 tablespoons milk
1¾ cups (11.5-ounce package) NESTLÉ® TOLL HOUSE®
  Milk Chocolate Morsels
1 cup quick or old-fashioned oats
½ cup raisins (optional)

PREHEAT oven to 375°F.

COMBINE flour, baking powder, baking soda, cinnamon and salt in small bowl. Beat butter, brown sugar, granulated sugar and vanilla extract in large mixer bowl until creamy. Beat in egg. Gradually beat in flour mixture and milk. Stir in morsels, oats and raisins. Drop by rounded tablespoon onto ungreased baking sheets.

BAKE for 10 to 14 minutes or until edges are crisp but centers are still soft. Cool on baking sheets for 2 minutes; remove to wire racks to cool completely.   *Makes about 3 dozen cookies*

When you have eaten and are satisfied, praise the
Lord . . . for the good land he has given you.
Deuteronomy 8:10 NIV

Sweet Potato Pecan Pie

1 (9-inch) prepared deep-dish pie crust

1½ cups pecan halves

½ cup light corn syrup

1 egg white

2 cups puréed cooked sweet potatoes (about 1½ pounds uncooked potatoes)

⅓ cup packed brown sugar

1 teaspoon vanilla

½ teaspoon ground cinnamon

¼ teaspoon salt

Pinch *each* ground nutmeg and ground cloves

2 eggs, beaten

1. Preheat oven to 400°F. Prick holes in bottom of pie crust with fork. Bake 10 minutes or until very lightly browned and dry; remove from oven. *Reduce oven temperature to 350°F.*

2. Combine pecans, corn syrup and egg white in small bowl; mix well. Set aside.

3. Combine sweet potatoes, brown sugar, vanilla, cinnamon, salt, nutmeg and cloves in large bowl; mix until well blended. Stir in eggs.

4. Spread sweet potato mixture in baked pie crust. Spoon pecan mixture evenly over top.

5. Bake 45 to 50 minutes or until filling is puffed and topping is golden. Cool completely on wire rack.   *Makes 8 servings*

Sweet potatoes do not need to be peeled but should be scrubbed under cold running water before cooking. They may be baked or boiled whole and then peeled and sliced or cubed.

The publisher would like to thank the companies and organizations listed below for the use of their recipes and photographs in this publication.

ACH Food Companies, Inc.

The Beef Checkoff

Bob Evans®

Campbell Soup Company

Dole Food Company, Inc.

Duncan Hines® and Moist Deluxe® are registered trademarks of Pinnacle Foods Corp.

The Hershey Company

Kraft Foods Global, Inc.

National Honey Board

Nestlé USA

Newman's Own, Inc.®

The Quaker® Oatmeal Kitchens

Reckitt Benckiser LLC.

Sargento® Foods Inc.

Unilever

USA Rice Federation®

VOLUME MEASUREMENTS (dry)

$\frac{1}{8}$ teaspoon = 0.5 mL
$\frac{1}{4}$ teaspoon = 1 mL
$\frac{1}{2}$ teaspoon = 2 mL
$\frac{3}{4}$ teaspoon = 4 mL
1 teaspoon = 5 mL
1 tablespoon = 15 mL
2 tablespoons = 30 mL
$\frac{1}{4}$ cup = 60 mL
$\frac{1}{3}$ cup = 75 mL
$\frac{1}{2}$ cup = 125 mL
$\frac{2}{3}$ cup = 150 mL
$\frac{3}{4}$ cup = 175 mL
1 cup = 250 mL
2 cups = 1 pint = 500 mL
3 cups = 750 mL
4 cups = 1 quart = 1 L

VOLUME MEASUREMENTS (fluid)

1 fluid ounce (2 tablespoons) = 30 mL
4 fluid ounces ($\frac{1}{2}$ cup) = 125 mL
8 fluid ounces (1 cup) = 250 mL
12 fluid ounces (1$\frac{1}{2}$ cups) = 375 mL
16 fluid ounces (2 cups) = 500 mL

WEIGHTS (mass)

$\frac{1}{2}$ ounce = 15 g
1 ounce = 30 g
3 ounces = 90 g
4 ounces = 120 g
8 ounces = 225 g
10 ounces = 285 g
12 ounces = 360 g
16 ounces = 1 pound = 450 g

DIMENSIONS

$\frac{1}{16}$ inch = 2 mm
$\frac{1}{8}$ inch = 3 mm
$\frac{1}{4}$ inch = 6 mm
$\frac{1}{2}$ inch = 1.5 cm
$\frac{3}{4}$ inch = 2 cm
1 inch = 2.5 cm

OVEN TEMPERATURES

250°F = 120°C
275°F = 140°C
300°F = 150°C
325°F = 160°C
350°F = 180°C
375°F = 190°C
400°F = 200°C
425°F = 220°C
450°F = 230°C

BAKING PAN SIZES

Utensil	Size in Inches/Quarts	Metric Volume	Size in Centimeters
Baking or Cake Pan (square or rectangular)	8×8×2	2 L	20×20×5
	9×9×2	2.5 L	23×23×5
	12×8×2	3 L	30×20×5
	13×9×2	3.5 L	33×23×5
Loaf Pan	8×4×3	1.5 L	20×10×7
	9×5×3	2 L	23×13×7
Round Layer Cake Pan	8×1½	1.2 L	20×4
	9×1½	1.5 L	23×4
Pie Plate	8×1¼	750 mL	20×3
	9×1¼	1 L	23×3
Baking Dish or Casserole	1 quart	1 L	—
	1½ quart	1.5 L	—
	2 quart	2 L	—